STOP PROCRASTINATING – RIGHT NOW!

Beat your procrastination habit once and for all

Written by Aurélie Dorchy

Translated by Jessica Foster

Health and Wellbeing 50MINUTES.com

STOP PROCRASTINATING – RIGHT NOW!   1

WHY DO I ALWAYS PUT THINGS OFF UNTIL LATER?   3

You are looking for perfection

You are afraid of disappointing someone

You need to control people

You are too confident in your own abilities

You refuse failure of any kind

You are afraid of success and of change

You work better under pressure

Other causes

The rituals of a procrastinator

HOW TO REDUCE YOUR PROCRASTINATION   13

Motivational thoughts

Organising your time

Manage your work

WHAT ATTITUDE SHOULD YOU ADOPT DURING YOUR PROGRESSION?   25

FAQS   27

Who are procrastinators?

Are procrastinators necessarily lazy? What are their attributes?

Why do we put off certain things until later?

When and how can we take back control of the situation?

Are there methods for managing my time better?

How can I reconcile unappealing tasks with personal enjoyment?

How can I help a procrastinator to improve their efficiency?

FURTHER READING 32

STOP PROCRASTINATING
– RIGHT NOW!

- **Problem:** some people find that, even though they want to do well, they always end up putting off certain tasks. Others may believe that they work better under pressure, while reality sometimes proves the opposite. Overcoming procrastination and getting things done is therefore a real challenge.
- **Aims:** take back control of your life and finally finish the projects that matter to you.
- **FAQs:**
  - Who are procrastinators?
  - Are procrastinators necessarily lazy? What are their attributes?
  - Why do we put off certain things until later?
  - When and how can we take back control of the situation?
  - Are there methods for managing my time better?
  - How can I reconcile unappealing tasks with personal enjoyment?
  - How can I help a procrastinator to improve their efficiency?

Nowadays, many people are affected by this problem, whether they be students, employees, artists, self-employed workers or retired. Indeed, who has never put something off until the next day because more enjoyable activities came up? The phenomenon is now so widespread that 25 March was declared International Procrastination Day in 2010. The problems arising from procrastination are linked to time management, a theme that has come to the forefront since the 1990s. This is because, in our society, doing nothing has no value, while mastering everything is idealised.

The causes and origins of procrastination are numerous and lead to all sorts of issues in our daily lives. A person who hates speaking on the phone will postpone urgent phone calls indefinitely, while a person who is terrified of success will never finish their thesis without being pushed to their limits by external circumstances. When we suffer from chronic procrastination, we feel worse and worse every day, even when we are avoiding our responsibilities by replacing them with more pleasant and reassuring tasks. The more time passes, the closer the deadline looms and the amount of work increases or seems even more stressful. Alongside this, we develop a sense of guilt around others.

When procrastination happens every day and the person in question does not take responsibility for it, it becomes a vicious circle which imprisons them and damages their self-esteem. But as well as these people who always put everything off until later, there are some people who do it less frequently and who would still like to improve their productivity or simply manage their time better so that they can enjoy their free time more. Whatever the reason, if you want to change, you need to start by becoming aware of your issues and accepting them. It is only once you have got through this stage that you will finally have the indispensable tools to a calmer daily life at your disposal. The solution is there...but you have to get to work right now!

WHY DO I ALWAYS PUT THINGS OFF UNTIL LATER?

Procrastination is experienced by many individuals and is caused by various fears. It can lead us to postpone a household chore or a long-term project, or even a complicated discussion with a loved one, indefinitely. The list of reasons for procrastination below is by no means exhaustive, but it reflects a great deal of the mental blocks that lead to procrastination. You might be affected by several or none of these; the important thing is to identify what is holding you back by considering all the possibilities. Deep down, you almost certainly know what it is, but you will undoubtedly be reassured to read that other people are experiencing the same dilemmas.

YOU ARE LOOKING FOR PERFECTION

Perfectionists cannot bear the idea of an ill-performed task. They know that when they start a job, particularly a long-term task or something they do not feel fully comfortable doing, they risk not doing it perfectly the first time and having to come back to it several times, without being sure that they will ever be satisfied with the result. In these conditions, doing nothing allows perfectionists to focus on easier tasks that they excel at, thus avoiding any potential disappointment. You should take care if you tend to work in this way, as striving for perfection risks halting rather than helping your progress.

"Perfection is the only way imaginable to me, I am not satisfied with average output, or even 'good enough' output; it can only be very good, and I would be even happier if it were exceptional. That is perhaps why I always put things off: I am afraid it will not be as good as my expectations. Nonetheless, I try to tell myself that if I don't work on it, it will never be good, and that should be enough motivation to get started; but no, it doesn't work." (Anita, 50)

YOU ARE AFRAID OF DISAPPOINTING SOMEONE

Someone who is afraid of letting down a thesis supervisor, an employer or a loved one, whether or not this is a consequence of perfectionism, probably does not feel up to the task that they must carry out or that has been entrusted to them. Thus, convinced that people think you have skills that you do not have or believe you do not have, you are not confident in your own abilities and you are afraid of seeing shock on the other person's face when they find out the scale of your incompetence. If you identify with this description, you might have impostor syndrome.

IMPOSTOR SYNDROME

People who suffer from impostor syndrome fear that someone will one day discover that they are not up to their job, that they are not as gifted as people thought and that they should be elsewhere. On account of this, they are hesitant to launch themselves into new projects that would show up their weaknesses and make them vulnerable in the eyes of others. In reality, they are doing the most harm to themselves, by needlessly limiting the development of their abilities.

Seeing yourself as an impostor surrounded by people whom you believe to be more competent, deserving or worthy, can lead to procrastination. Thus, to avoid other people being disappointed in you, you endlessly postpone whatever you have to do. Yet, by putting a task off indefinitely, you are reinforcing the feeling that you are an impostor and heading straight for self-sabotage.

It is important to be aware that everyone is vulnerable and susceptible to mistakes, without this affecting who we are. No one is expecting you to do everything perfectly the first time. Forget what other people think and simply do your best.

YOU NEED TO CONTROL PEOPLE

Always being late to meetings and regularly missing project deadlines without feeling guilty could be due to a subconscious need to control other people. Someone who behaves in this way clearly cannot bear the limits imposed on them by other people, whether they are peers or superiors. A desire for freedom and control of their time is a contributing factor here.

Accepting that others define part of our priorities and our time can be difficult, because we think that we alone are in charge of our lives. Yet, while it is true that we should not accept everything from other people, it is sometimes necessary to obey deadlines set by other people in order to successfully complete certain projects. This is particularly true in a professional setting where, unless you are your own boss, not accepting fixed deadlines can cost you dearly.

YOU ARE TOO CONFIDENT IN YOUR OWN ABILITIES

Some procrastinators, who are too confident in their own abilities, do not take the specific problems of each new task into account. When everything has always gone well, it is difficult to imagine that things will not necessarily happen as they should. This person risks misunderstanding the scale of the job, its difficulty or the time required to accomplish a new project. Unconsciously, however, it will seem to them that they are playing with fire and they might feel as though they are on a slippery slope. It is therefore important to be aware of your abilities, but also of the specific characteristics pertaining to the task that you are required to accomplish.

> "When things are difficult, I also put them off for as long as possible, telling myself I will work on them later and during the days after that. Thus the work piles up, and as the time allowed to do it is decreasing, stress gradually increases." (Justine, 35)

YOU REFUSE FAILURE OF ANY KIND

Strongly linked to perfectionism and the fear of disappointing people, fear of failure motivates many people to put off projects that they care about. In this way, if they are not successful, it will only be because not much time was spent on them, and not because the person in question was incapable of managing the files. This is actually less destabilising than having worked for hours for nothing.

However, it is by leaving our comfort zones that we can discover new skills and evolve. Facing up to the difficulties we encounter allows us to know ourselves better and to overcome our fears.

YOU ARE AFRAID OF SUCCESS AND OF CHANGE

While some people are more afraid of failure than anything else, others, on the contrary, unconsciously try to avoid success, after which they are sure they will be chosen for increasingly important projects. In reality, they are terrified by the idea of being in the spotlight, growing, developing and being in control of their own lives. These procrastinators struggle to imagine themselves in the future; that is why they prefer to spend their time on well-defined, even repetitive tasks that they are familiar with. They remain stuck in their comfort zone, and never dare to do anything that would make them step outside of it.

However, actively working on our fears and anxieties allows us to grow. The possibilities for evolving that present themselves are sometimes less frightening than we imagined and are an opportunity to use our skills in more exciting challenges and to truly learn something.

YOU WORK BETTER UNDER PRESSURE

Although it can be exhilarating to stay up for nights on end to finish a project because you did not start it early enough, this way of working always carries a risk and can even end up being catastrophic in some cases. A person who works under pressure always wonders if this time they will manage to finish what they have to do in the allowed time, which is extremely stressful.

So even if you think you need adrenaline to progress, and even if you know that you will be even more proud to have finished your work before the deadline, this type of behaviour risks becoming exhausting quickly. In addition, constantly working under pressure inevitably means that some aspects of the project will have to be neglected due to a lack of time. It can be very frustrating to realise that you could have done much better if you had set to work earlier.

OTHER CAUSES

Other fears can be behind procrastination. While some people lack long-term vision and do not notice what could help them finish a task, preferring to prioritise whatever will give them immediate satisfaction, others are afraid of losing free time or being chained to their desk. For some people, making decisions will always be the obstacle that stops them in their tracks, due to fear of the impact these decisions could have on their futures and the impossibility of turning back. Others will simply refuse to undertake a project that might be costly to them and will put all their effort into smaller tasks with quicker results.

All these problems illustrate how important it is to reflect on our own limits and identify the main ones, so that we can question them and reduce the issues they cause. If, deep down, you want to move mountains or simply better organise yourself, it would be a pity not to work on the causes of your procrastination to finally take control of your own life.

TEST: IDENTIFY WHAT IS STOPPING YOU FROM TAKING ACTION

From the following statements, choose the ones that you identify with most and count the number of a)s, b)s and c)s you have.

a) Prioritising tasks is difficult for me.
b) I am very sensitive to what other people think.
b) I feel worthless when I fail at something.
c) As long as I don't make a decision, I can stay in my comfort zone.
c) I cannot bear criticism.
a) I need encouragement to start working.
a) I do not believe I am very methodical.
c) I refuse to listen to orders.
b) Nothing I do seems good enough to me.
a) I often see the projects I am given as unachievable.
b) I pay great attention to detail.
c) I always miss deadlines.
b) When demands seem too high to me, I rush things and mess them up.

a) I am more interested in something that can bring me immediate satisfaction.

a) I always think I have enough time, so I do nothing, and I end up having to do everything under pressure.

b) I need a lot of acknowledgement to progress.

c) I try to do everything by myself, without help from anyone else.

c) I am afraid of seeming vulnerable.

b) I think I am less intelligent than those around me.

b) Responsibility makes me anxious.

a) I do not feel pressured by tasks with a far-off deadline.

c) I avoid doing tasks that are not in line with my logical and creative spirit.

b) I am very sensitive to negative criticism.

c) I am often late to work, meetings or social commitments.

a) When I have to do something, I never know where to start.

a) When I have an objective in mind, it is easy to move away from my task.

b) I do not have confidence in my abilities.

c) I do not want people to notice my faults.

c) I do not start a project if I am not sure that I will be successful.

a) If I do not fully understand the work that needs to be done, I leave it.

Results:

- **Mostly a)s:** I lack method. The reason I regularly put tasks off is mainly because I am not very methodical or because I do not fully understand the task at hand. I therefore concentrate on what I know well or whatever brings immediate satisfaction. Allowing time for reflection, however, often yields solutions to problems that could arise during a task.

- **Mostly b)s:** I am afraid of letting people down. The fear of disappointing people often goes hand in hand with a lack of self-confidence. It can be the consequence of too high expectations of oneself or simply related to wanting to please everyone around us to achieve a certain legitimacy. These thoughts prevent us from undertaking projects that risk exposing us to criticism. However, it is by undertaking these projects that we can acquire new skills and perfect our existing abilities.
- **Mostly c)s:** I want to be in control. By constantly arriving late or opposing orders, I give the impression of wanting to control everything and being the only person who decides on my schedule. I probably cannot stand criticism and prefer to spend time on activities that give me full satisfaction. While it is true that fully managing one's time has certain attractions, it is impossible, however, to ignore others. Why not negotiate so that everyone can find what works for them?

THE RITUALS OF A PROCRASTINATOR

A procrastinator has several rituals for avoiding unenjoyable tasks. These are the three main ones:

- they put them off to a more opportune moment;
- they designate another activity as more important;
- they claim not to have time.

Unlike the numerous causes that explain procrastination, the way in which it translates into real life is not as diversified: you choose to focus on something else, you lie, you pretend to forget; in short, you put it off!

HOW TO REDUCE YOUR PROCRASTINATION

MOTIVATIONAL THOUGHTS

Ask yourself the right questions

Regularly ask yourself if your activities are well and truly linked to your life goals. If they are too distant, it is normal that you will not want to spend time on them. Sometimes, however, upon reflection, it is possible to find an aspect of the task at hand that is beneficial to you. If you cannot find one, perhaps it is time for you to start asking yourself about your choice of career of some of your life choices.

Resist temptation

If some activities, on the other hand, are important to you, but fairly difficult to carry out, you must first of all imagine yourself in the future and think about how difficult it would be to live with the harmful consequences of having done nothing. If you never pay your rent on time, imagine your landlord kicking you out, for example.

Secondly, you need to identify the temptations that could distract you from your objective. Of course, the aim is not to ban them completely, but to increase your ability to resist them. This could be films, social events, social networks, video games, or even chores which can become an attractive temptation when they might distract us from a complex task.

Reducing temptation is not easy, which is why it must be done gradually. It is by progressing step by step that you will see the most improvement. Identify the times of day during which you are most likely to be distracted. If you are not particularly efficient in the evening, for example, do not schedule important and complex tasks for this time. Rather, take advantage of this time to do the tasks that annoy you the least. When you have made good progress on a difficult project, reward yourself with a short break during which you can do exactly what you want.

It is also important to analyse what you are doing to figure out what you like doing the most. If, for example, you spend a lot of time on the internet, browsing between sites, why not choose the ones that usually distract you and set aside a period of time during which you can look at them each day? Do not try to stop all these time-wasting activities in one go. This risks not being as conclusive as you would like it to be and this could discourage you in your efforts.

Equally, it is also important to find pleasure and happiness in the completion of your projects. Aren't you actually happier when you finish something you had to do than when you are simply watching a film?

Be your own best friend

In the fight against procrastination, you are the most capable of knowing what works for you. And what would happen if you decided from now on to believe in yourself and to give yourself the best support possible in completing your projects? If one of your friends was struggling in this way, what would you do for them? Would you belittle them until they ended up giving up or, on the contrary, would you encourage them to finish what they had started?

The second attitude is the one we encourage you to adopt for yourself. To help you gain confidence, you could, for example, write down three positive things that you have done during the day in a notebook and look at it from time to time for motivation.

ORGANISING YOUR TIME

Divide your tasks up into smaller activities

When you have to complete a task, whether professional or to do with your personal life, it is a good idea to divide the task into several sub-tasks. If, for example, you have to work on a writing project, mark out the sections of text that you want to work on each day. 'Write thesis' becomes 'Write point A', 'Write point B', and so on, even 'Write the first paragraph of point A'.

Be precise! The more sub-tasks in a task, the more doable it will seem, and it will be even easier to manage your time. Moreover, this will allow you to immediately know what you have to do, and you will not be able to find ritual distractions to avoid your mission for the day.

Make lists

Making a list of things to do is the most popular and effective technique for organising your day as well as possible. To do this, it is always advisable to mix easy tasks with tasks that are the least enjoyable to you. Once you have listed all your activities, consider dividing them in a way that suits you and rank them according to their priority: some will be urgent and important (UI), others urgent and not important (Ui), others not urgent but important (uI) and, finally, those that are neither urgent nor important (ui). This ordering technique, suggested by Daniel Latrobe in his book on time management, will help you to identify what you really have to focus your energy on and what you should make a priority.

To-do list: not organised		To-do list: organised	
First of all, write out everything you want to achieve in the day. Then give each task a grade of urgency and importance.		Next, reorganise your schedule in the most logical way you can. You will immediately see what absolutely needs to be done and what can take a back seat.	
☐ Drive children to school	UI	UI	☐ Drive children to school
☐ Organise daughter's surprise party	uI	UI	☐ Go grocery shopping
☐ Make lunch	Ui	UI	☐ Collect children from school at 1pm
☐ Read a book	ui	Ui	☐ Make lunch
☐ Do an hour of exercise	uI	uI	☐ Organise daughter's surprise party
☐ Collect children from school at 1pm	UI	uI	☐ Do an hour of exercise
☐ Catch up with Peter	ui	ui	☐ Read a book
☐ Go grocery shopping	UI	ui	☐ Catch up with Peter

These lists must be shown visibly in your environment so that you can always see them. This will allow you to keep your objective in sight. Feel free to change their appearance so that they are attractive to you.

When a task is finished, get into the habit of crossing it off your list. As such, you will be aware of your progress and will derive more pleasure and motivation from it.

If you want to have an exact idea of what you have to do and plan it into your day, choose the time-organised list. The more overwhelmed you are, the more this technique will be useful for refocusing you and preventing you from spending too much time on one task at the expense of another. Do not forget, however, that you are not a machine, and overly busy days must be avoided as much as possible.

The time-organised list that we suggest here is for someone who wants to reconcile family life, personal projects and housework. If you use a similar system, make sure to allocate longer time slots than necessary, in order to handle unexpected circumstances or tiredness that might arise.

Time-organised list

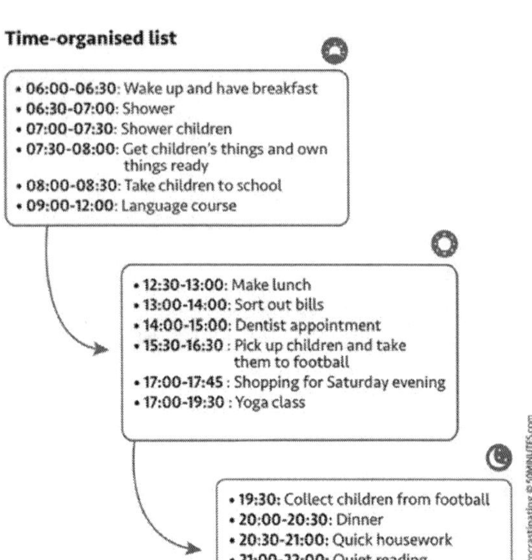

Using a reverse schedule

When you know the end date by which you need to have finished a large project, you need to create a reverse schedule. Unlike the simple lists that you have to write up on a daily basis and that give a view of the tasks you must do precisely on that day, a reverse schedule offers an overall view of a given period of time (a month, a term, a year, etc.).

Start from the date of your event or deadline and work

backwards in time. In this table, write the stages of your project and specify the time necessary to their completion. It is important to allow for margins of error, as correctly evaluating the duration of an action is not easy, and unforeseen circumstances can always arise.

The reverse schedule suggested below is related to the preparation of a surprise birthday party on 4 June 2016. The different things to organise are divided into several tasks, of which the completion could take several days. Do not forget to always leave a little extra time to deal with unforeseen circumstances. The stages that will contribute to creating a special atmosphere for the birthday are in blue and the more general tasks, such as getting a caterer, etc. are in pink.

Organising Natalie's birthday party (4 June 2016)

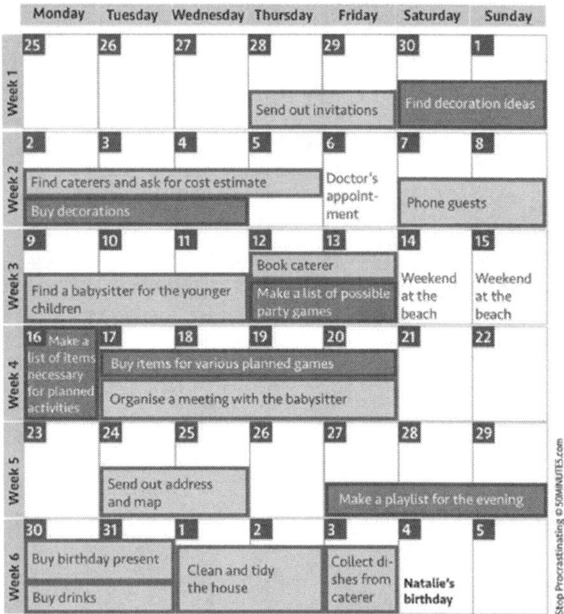

The use of a Gantt diagram is often required for an effective reverse schedule, as it allows us to immediately visualise the division of tasks, their progress, etc. The premise is simple, but writing it can take some time. It involves listing the concrete tasks to undertake for a specific project, predicting a duration for each of them and making this information (tasks/duration) visible in a table. During the accomplishment of these tasks, the bars representing durations will be filled in.

Gantt reverse schedule

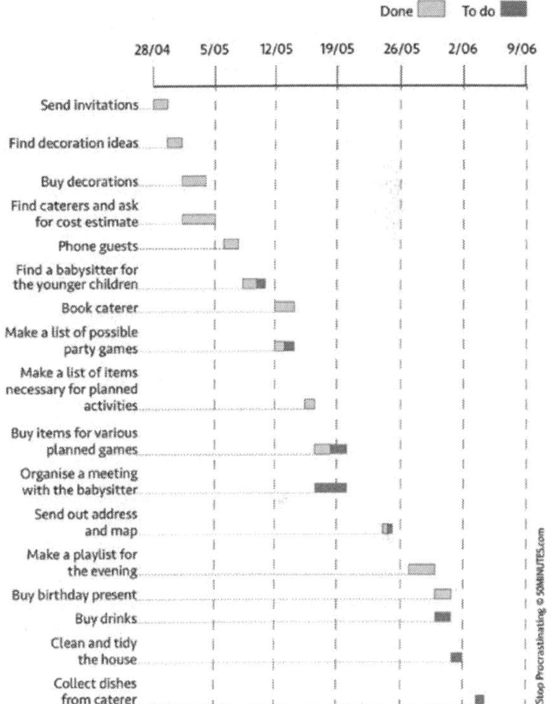

Plan your leisure time

Planning your leisure time will avoid you spending too long on it during the week, or ignoring it in favour of your duties. For certain people, this method might lack spontaneity, but it will nonetheless ensure that you have time slots dedicated to what you really enjoy doing.

The Pomodoro Technique®

Invented by the Italian Francesco Cirillo in the late 1980s, while he was still a student, the Pomodoro Technique® consists of planning work sessions of 25 minutes, interspersed with 5-minute breaks. At the end of four work sessions (4 x 25 minutes plus 4 x 5 minutes), you can reward yourself with a 15-minute break. The aim is to constantly revitalise your concentration to stay focused and give yourself a better idea of how long it takes to complete a task. The creator of the method invites its users to calculate the necessary duration for each task in "pomodori" rather than in an amount of time.

> ### DID YOU KNOW?
>
> *Pomodoro* means 'tomato' in Italian. This name comes from the tomato-shaped kitchen timer used by the method's inventor to monitor his 25-minute sessions.

Some ideas for making the most of your short breaks:

- Go out and walk around a little;
- Do some stretching;
- Meditate;
- Read a newspaper article;
- Drink a glass of water or a coffee;
- Eat a snack (preferably fruit);
- Do a short household chore;
- Etc.

MANAGE YOUR WORK

Choose a suitable location

For you to be able to complete your tasks as well as possible, it is important to find a location that is conducive to the type of activity that you want to carry out. Do you need to concentrate? Go to a calm place where no one will disturb you. If you are interrupted by someone, feel free to unashamedly tell them that you are busy, and agree on another time to talk.

Start with whatever seems the most difficult

After listing the things you have to do during the day, it is often preferable to start with the one that will require the most energy, either intellectually or physically. Do not forget that we tend to have more energy in the morning than in the afternoon, when tiredness linked to digestion can be felt. Once this task is finished, you will be able to visualise the rest of the day more calmly.

Get into the habit of taking action directly

As soon as you have an idea about a project or you decide you want to do something, because you feel inspired or because it would be a good time to do it, jump straight into action. Putting off this task will force you to deal with it later, when the inspiration is long gone and other duties will have been added to your to-do list.

Delegate when possible

Sometimes, it is good to accept and ask for the help of those around us if we think we cannot finish our list of tasks. Nonetheless, you should be aware of the tasks the person you wish to delegate to is busy with and you should not impose your way of working on them. Make sure that you respect everyone's schedules and take their priorities and needs into account.

WHAT ATTITUDE SHOULD YOU ADOPT DURING YOUR PROGRESSION?

As you know, changing your behaviour takes time and moderating your procrastination requires a certain amount of work on yourself. You will therefore have to persevere, which implies accepting that you will have to constantly question yourself. Even if you happen to regularly concede to distractions at the beginning, you will be able to gradually limit yourself to concentrating on what truly interests you through daily awareness.

As we are all different, feel free to test the various techniques suggested, according to your desires and needs. When you figure out what works best for you, feel free to use a more personalised time management system. Be creative too. If you dislike creating Excel spreadsheets for your schedule, write it on paper or find other applications that will allow you to organise your time in a more attractive way.

Thanks to the progress you make, your self-confidence will improve, as well as your ability to evaluate the necessary time to undertake a task. While you may have had pre-conceptions as to the difficulty of a task, truly dedicating your time to it by using the strategies suggested here will help you to realise that they do not require as much time or energy as you thought. You will no longer be afraid to get on with them. By working on your motivation and against the various things that are blocking you, you will not only resolve an organisational problem, but you will also become aware of the desire that motivates you and allows you to deal with different situations. Taking action will become easier.

FAQS

WHO ARE PROCRASTINATORS?

Procrastinators can be anyone, including you and me. When someone tends to put off certain tasks, they are procrastinating. There are clearly many different types of procrastinator: those who always postpone doing anything and never take charge of things, making them lazy procrastinators; there are those who hide behind a pile of simple tasks so that they do not have to do whatever they find the most difficult or complex, in which case they are structured procrastinators; etc. The issue concerns such a vast number of people that an entire day has been dedicated to it.

ARE PROCRASTINATORS NECESSARILY LAZY? WHAT ARE THEIR ATTRIBUTES?

Procrastinators are not necessarily lazy – on the contrary! They can even prove themselves to be very active by dealing with many obligations. What differentiates them from other people is that they tend to focus on things of secondary importance. That is why, if you suffer from this, it is important to learn to classify daily tasks according to their priority and to stick to this.

Despite the problems that procrastination can cause, it can also help the development of certain qualities. In fact, procrastinators often have to be creative in finding solutions in order to meet looming deadlines that they are faced with. Additionally, being able to work effectively under pressure can be a significant asset in many jobs. Finally, procrastinating sometimes allows an idea to develop or original sources of inspiration to be found which would not have been uncovered otherwise.

WHY DO WE PUT OFF CERTAIN THINGS UNTIL LATER?

The reasons for doing this are different and specific to each individual. Some people are afraid of not doing a perfect job, others of missing out on free time, and many people of failing or even succeeding. By taking a step back, you can find the main reason for your own procrastination and work on it. Accept it and work on it regularly, without judging yourself, in order to improve gradually.

WHEN AND HOW CAN WE TAKE BACK CONTROL OF THE SITUATION?

When you feel like you are not managing your time well, or simply when your tendency to always do everything at the last minute has caused you harm. Firstly, you need to determine the obstacles and recurring difficulties that often stand in your way, and find a way of overcoming your fears and channelling your emotions. At the same time, or subsequently, be aware of the tricks that exist for becoming more productive. Working on this regularly is essential for fixing new habits in your life in the long term, in the same way as it is for acquiring new skills.

ARE THERE METHODS FOR MANAGING MY TIME BETTER?

There are many methods, or rather little ways of motivating yourself to do the most complex and exhausting tasks. Some are tried and tested, others are more original and just need you to develop and personalise them. The list method is the most classic, but it will not always be enough to keep up your motivation. Therefore, feel free to try out several to find the one that suits you best.

HOW CAN I RECONCILE UNAPPEALING TASKS WITH PERSONAL ENJOYMENT?

By allowing yourself to alternate work and pleasure, as well as making your work something you like doing, you will start to enjoy the tasks that you are busy with every day. As that is not always possible, simply connect what is useful with what is enjoyable. You can easily do the ironing or washing up while listening to music or watching a film, for example. If you find exercising boring, think of the benefits that will come from your efforts, but also the positive aspects of the course itself.

It is also very important to give your mind a break from time to time by taking breaks to allow new ideas to shine through, and to rediscover your motivation. That does not mean, however, that you can do any old thing during these moments of relaxation. Choose activities that can really change your thinking. Why not go for a walk for twenty minutes rather than sitting in front of the television?

HOW CAN I HELP A PROCRASTINATOR TO IMPROVE THEIR EFFICIENCY?

To help a procrastinator to be more efficient, you have to support them and not blame them. Feel free to offer to help in writing up a schedule or completing a few tasks together. You might have skills that they do not and that could help them to see the problem in a new light. You could offer to 'confiscate', if they agree, some sources of distraction in order to help them concentrate; or suggest that they report their progress on the project that they are working on. This will allow them to see the progress they have made and to feel supported.

We want to hear from you!
Leave a comment on your online library
and share your favourite books on social media!

FURTHER READING

BIBLIOGRAPHY

- Cirillo, F. (2012) *The Pomodoro Technique*. Berlin: FC Garage GmbH.
- Ferrari, M. (2014) *Stop à la procrastination, c'est malin. Allez enfin au bout de vos projets*. Paris, Quotidien Malin, 2014.
- Latrobe, D. (2000) *Gérer efficacement son temps et ses priorités. Concilier efficacité et bien-être*. Issy-les-Moulineaux: ESF Éditeur.
- Perry, J. (2012) *The Art of Procrastination: The Art of Effective Dawdling, Dallying, Lollygagging, and Postponing*. New York: Workman.
- LePoint.fr (2013) *Etes-vous un procrastinateur ?* [Online]. [Accessed 29 February 2016]. Available from: <http://www.lepoint.fr/societe/etes-vous-un-procrastina-teur-06-06-2013-1688525_23.php>

ADDITIONAL SOURCES

- Burka, J. and Yuen, L. (2008) *Procrastination: Why You Do It, What to Do About It Now*. Boston: Da Capo.
- Steel, P. (2011) *The Procrastination Equation: How to Stop Putting Things Off and Start Getting Stuff Done*. Harlow: Pearson.

IMPROVE YOUR GENERAL KNOWLEDGE

IN A BLINK OF AN EYE !

www.50minutes.com

www.50minutes.com

Ebook EAN: 9782806288981

Paperback EAN: 9782806288998

Legal Deposit: D/2016/12603/732

Cover: © Primento

Digital conception by Primento, the digital partner of publishers.

Made in the USA
Monee, IL
07 July 2026